I0405314

Video Marketing Works
...If You Work It!

Leveraging YouTube videos to market your business
and generate real leads!

HOWARD HALE

Video Marketing Absolutely Works!

As a business owner, it's important to understand the value of video and what it can do for your business.

Creating videos to tell your story is as paramount as having a phone number for your potential customer, clients and patients to connect with you, buy your products or services, and engage with you on a much deeper level.

If you need more leads and you are thinking about leveraging video for your business, then you're reading the right book!

Written by Howard Hale
Editing by Sarah Weeks
Cover Design by Tri Widyatmaka

Copyright © 2015 by Howard Hale
ISBN: 978-1-5053-8789-6

Will Video Work For Your Business?

One of the questions I get all the time: Will this work for my business? I have created literally thousands of websites and hundreds of videos. I have yet to meet a business that I can't help out with video.

Here are some of the businesses I've worked with:

Advertising Firms
Architectural Firms
Attorneys
Authors
Chiropractors
Clothing Companies
Coffee Companies
Consultants
Contractors
Dentists
Design Firms
Educators
Fertility Clinics
Industrial Firms
Insurance Agents

Landscapers
Manufactures
Music Instructors
Naturopaths
Non-Profit Groups
Packaging Companies
Pharmaceutical Companies
Physicians
Plumbers
Real Estate Agents
Retail Companies
Software Companies
Travel

I think you get the picture. Yes, it will work for you!

Foreword

Why video? Video has become the most effective way to generate the greatest number of leads for the least amount of money. In fact, video has become so affordable and compelling that some of my clients are literally creating dozens of videos to capture leads for their business.

It's also become a necessity for all businesses with or without websites to create videos. Video can translate your company's brand and compel viewers to pick up the phone or purchase from your website in seconds.

Videos can appeal to both the auditory and visual areas of our brain and make a more lasting impression and certainly more vividly than just text from your website, blog or Facebook post.

Video has the power to translate wordy and complicated concepts and subjects into stories that are not only entertaining but easier for consumers to digest.

This is the reason why websites featuring videos engage potential visitors and convert them into sales. I've discovered how to create effective videos, have them rank high in Google searches, and generate real leads – creating income that far exceeds what you can make from other forms of online marketing!

Part of the secret to video marketing and its success is

that video has the ability to be a standalone marketing tool and at the same time, can be integrated into all other forms of online marketing.

Videos have become the #1 tactic for traffic and lead generation.

Check out these statistics from YouTube. If you haven't seen these, then you are in for an eye opener!

- More than 1 billion unique users visit YouTube each month
- Over 6 billion hours of video are watched each month on YouTube – that's almost an hour for every person on Earth
- 100 hours of video are uploaded to YouTube every minute
- 80% of YouTube traffic comes from outside the US
- YouTube is localized in 61 countries and across 61 languages
- According to Nielsen, YouTube reaches more US adults ages 18-34 than any cable network

As a business owner, you need to see video as a viable resource for leads and new customers. This book will also help you discover how to track the effectiveness of videos and create what's called a conversion ratio. That's the cost of the videos divided by the number of leads; we will go into more detail about this later on.

As you read on, you will discover the power of video and how you can leverage it for your business!

Contents

ACKNOWLEDGEMENTS

Thank you to my past, present and future clients. Words cannot express how grateful I am for your trust in all that I do to market your business.

To our future success!

Cheers,

Howard Hale

Howard Hale

INTRODUCTION
THE IMPORTANCE OF VIDEO FOR SMALL BUSINESSES

When I create videos for my clients I do so with the
intention of providing invaluable information to their
potential customers, clients or patients. This information
is either delivered for the sake of informing consumers
or to engage them in a way that compels them to
purchase your product or services. Either way, videos
help websites and all other online marketing tactics to
accomplish this goal more efficiently.

In addition to that, videos can help your website capture
more traffic and enhance the conversion process. This
has been proven statistically by tracking the drop off
rate. (a.k.a. bounce rate). The drop off rate indicates how
long the user stayed on the website. If the user does not
find anything of interest, they bounce or drop off the
website.

Statistics show that videos can dramatically reduce your
bounce rate and increase engagement. The traffic that
videos generate is usually more relevant and results in
generating revenue through online purchases or a phone
call to the company directly.   (Remember that your
strategy should included your intention regarding how
you want visitors to connect with your business. Some
companies only want online sales, and some only want
phone calls.)

Call for FREE 20 minute video consultation: 1-866-900-6969
Want to shoot your own videos? www.SmartPhoneVideoToolkit.com

1

Videos can affect page rankings. Websites that have videos are given priority, and thus they naturally rank high in searches. Moreover, videos are also shared on social media sites and other media platforms. Think about it: when was the last time one of your webpages was re-posted on a social site?

How does video benefit businesses?
Clearly, evolving trends have made it mandatory for businesses to have video.

If you are marketing your product with text, then your audience will understand what you are selling and why, but they won't be able to grasp the feeling of your business. On the contrary, videos, despite being small and concise, will deliver your brand's identity. Videos can deliver all the how's, what's and why's regarding the brand (provided that your storyline is strong) in just seconds. They will help you convey to your customer the 'experience,' which is a very strong marketing tool!

There is another reason why videos generate more traffic and are admired by people. They motivate interaction between people, even though they're virtual. A person who is watching the video can see and hear what your business has to say. They can see your business representatives, business owner, happy customers, and get a feel for what it would be like to be your customer. The main communication bond is established with the help of body language. People don't always say what they mean, but their body language radiates a sense or feeling about your company and its brand.

Call for FREE 20 minute video consultation: 1-866-900-6969
Want to shoot your own videos? www.SmartPhoneVideoToolkit.com

2

You personally don't have to be on camera!
If you don't want to be on camera, there are many ways to create effective videos without having to be in front of the camera. I will explain how later on in the book, so read on if you know you need videos and are camera shy. In fact, I'd suggest that if you have people in your organization who are not willing participants that you not force them to be. Being on camera is a lot like public speaking; you either thrive on it or you don't. Whatever side of the fence you reside on is OK. We have strategies that will engage your consumer and convey your company's message.

Some of your videos could be divided into two primary categories. The first type is relationship videos, which inform the users what's new about the business, how they can get in touch with the business, and what benefits they can expect. These types of videos usually focus on establishing customer relationships. The other and most common type is marketing videos. These videos focus solely on increasing the sales of the business by generating leads and telling the visitor how they can go about connecting with your business and or purchasing products or services.

If you want your business to turn into a brand name, then you need to have a representation in the form of video. By reading this book you are one step ahead of your competition, and if you follow some of the strategies outlined here, you can gain significant advantage over your competition. Videos can dramatically simplify this task for you!

Call for FREE 20 minute video consultation: 1-866-900-6969
Want to shoot your own videos? www.SmartPhoneVideoToolkit.com

3

1
HOW DO YOU KNOW VIDEO WORKS?
TRACKING YOUR SUCCESS IS THE KEY!

"Business decision makers LOVE online video because it gives them the most amount of information in the shortest amount of time." – Robert Weiss

The questions I get most frequently are: "How do I know it's working?" and "Why should I trust video on my website?" Those are both relevant and important questions!

Let's start with trust. First, test it out for yourself. Type the search term, "Video Marketing Woodinville" into Google. This is the community in which I live, and as you can see, my video shows up on the first page of Google. More than likely, it's pretty close to the top.

Image that your customer, clients or patients are doing a search and your business video shows up on the first page of Google. What link do you think they are most likely to click on? OK, I've already quoted the statistic that videos generate a 45% higher click-through rate than regular text links. But once you look at it in this context, it's pretty easy to see that video can make a huge difference in your bottom line, and it tells your

Call for FREE 20 minute video consultation: 1-866-900-6969
Want to shoot your own videos? www.SmartPhoneVideoToolkit.com

4

story faster than any other means.

The first question, "How do I know it's working?" is even more important to understand. Imagine you have multiple marketing campaigns all going at the same time. As an example, you have one video, a small newspaper ad, your website, and maybe a Google Pay-Per-Click ad. How do you know which ones are working and which ones are not? Some of my clients are really good about tracking: when the consumer calls, they ask them. But it's not 100% foolproof. Sometimes your potential consumers just say they saw you on the internet and can't remember where. So when it comes to tracking the effectiveness of your marketing campaigns, asking your consumers is NOT foolproof.

Using a call tracking numbers is the #1 thing you can do to ensure you are spending your marketing dollars wisely
About 5 years ago, I had a client who was heavily into using the phone book for advertising, and in fact spent over 7 figures at one time on the Yellow Pages. I knew that I had to track the effectiveness (or lack thereof) of the method he used, in comparison to the effectiveness of online marketing that I ran for him. The problem was, he had several different business names, ran many campaigns simultaneously, and didn't have a metric other than a guess or feel as to how well these campaigns were running.

You don't have to have a big budget to save a lot of money using a tracking number
I decided to assign a tracking number to every one of my campaigns. I had tracking numbers for websites, videos, small print ads in newspapers, church bulletins, coupon

Call for FREE 20 minute video consultation: 1-866-900-6969
Want to shoot your own videos? www.SmartPhoneVideoToolkit.com

5

advertising, city-based landing pages, Google Places listings, periodicals, and Pay-Per-Click ads on landing pages. Once I did this, each month I was able to see in an easy-to-read bar chart exactly which campaigns were working and which ones were not. I had irrefutable proof that the Yellow Pages were no longer effective, and in fact were costing us $297 per phone call! That's right, I used call tracking numbers and did a report on all the calls we got. I divided by the number of calls and we spent almost $300 for just a phone call – not even a sale, just a call! When I compared that to all of our other forms of marketing, we spent a fraction of that on each of those. What's more important is that call tracking allowed me to show this to all the vendors, so that they could see the results we got from their advertising, and it helped me negotiate their rates down. If they didn't negotiate and our cost per acquisition was above a certain threshold, then we ended our contract with them.

There is no substitute for knowing exactly what your customers cost
The other point I'd like to drive home is that call tracking numbers are $5 each, and you only need one for each campaign. If you're wasting hundreds or thousands of dollars on a campaign, how would you know? With a call tracking number you can set your reports for daily, weekly or monthly and make intelligent decisions based on how many calls you are getting. You can reallocate your financial resources to campaigns or ads that are working and quit ones that are not!

There are several call tracking companies and they all provide a variety of other services that are invaluable to

Call for FREE 20 minute video consultation: 1-866-900-6969
Want to shoot your own videos? www.SmartPhoneVideoToolkit.com

6

the small business person. Kall8.com and CallFire.com are two of the more popular companies. If yo u need help or a deeper understanding about call tracking numbers, please feel free to contact me on how to set this up. It's really quite easy!

Call for FREE 20 minute video consultation: 1-866-900-6969
Want to shoot your own videos? www.SmartPhoneVideoToolkit.com

7

2
TYPES OF VIDEO

"Humans are incredibly visual and powerful, moving images help us find meaning... [and] video helps capture and contextualize the world around us." – Dan Patterson

What type of video should you start with? What's the specific purpose of each type of video? The answers to these two questions are important to know. Some videos are solely designed to educate, while others are there to lead new customers into your sales funnel and generate revenue. Videos can be loosely divided into four types. Let's see what they are and where can they be used.

1. Promotional Video
As evident from the name, promotional videos are used for advertising and campaigning purposes. These videos do not require high end equipment, but if you have some, do not refrain from using them. The main purpose of these videos is to deliver the information about the brand and what services and advantages people can acquire if they hire or purchase these services.

Here are a few points that can help you in the making of promotional videos.

- **Know Your Target Audience** – Every product

Call for FREE 20 minute video consultation: 1-866-900-6969
Want to shoot your own videos? www.SmartPhoneVideoToolkit.com

8

or service is designed for a specific audience. If you have conducted some research before designing the marketing strategy of your brand, then you must know the age group of your target audience. You will want to make your promotional videos from the point of view of that age group. The storyline, actors and theme should all be in accordance with the mindset of the target audience; only then will you be able to inspire your audience to share your videos.

- **Video Elements** – You know which age group to play to. Now the question is: what is the best way to deliver the information? Should it feature images and narration, or should you hire actors to present a story? This depends on your budget. If you have a small budget, then you can hire a narrator, otherwise it's best to go with a scripted performance, which is more compelling.

- **Music and Other Miscellaneous Features** – Custom graphics, music and images enhance the visual quality of a video. If you are not hiring a professional video maker, then naturally you won't be able to incorporate these features in your video. Otherwise, you can use all these additional features to make a video more compelling. Again, make sure that these elements are in accordance with the taste of your target audience.

2. Outreach Video

Outreach videos are designed for a cause or purpose, and they are targeted towards a certain community. Most of these videos are for public service messages, but some brands treat them as a marketing tool as well.

Call for FREE 20 minute video consultation: 1-866-900-6969
Want to shoot your own videos? www.SmartPhoneVideoToolkit.com

9

These videos can be used to inform the public about a disease, an event, or newly-launched product or service. An NGO might use an outreach video to create awareness about a calamity. An event management business can use outreach videos to create a buzz about an event, and a lawyer can use these videos to drive a campaign. Thus, different people use it for different purposes.

Outreach videos don't necessarily have to be flashy, with animation or cool graphics; they can be simple photo slideshows with music. The reason you don't need to have visually attractive features in these videos is that the audience knows and has been pulled in by the subject even before they hit the play button. They know that the video is intended to create awareness among a certain group of people, and it will be focused on delivering the message to the audience rather than indulging in pleasantries.

If you are making outreach videos, then make sure you are stating your message clearly. You need to be succinct because people won't wait for you to come to the point. The percentage of people who watch serious videos is comparatively small, and if you want to get through to them, you need to take care with timing.

3. How-To Video
This is the most popular category of videos, and the one that generates the most traffic. These videos are visual tutorials that tell the viewers how something is done. How-to videos can also create sales and are a perfect opportunity to upsell and introduce new products to your current customer base. I'd suggest putting these towards the end of your video; these are called outtros.

Call for FREE 20 minute video consultation: 1-866-900-6969
Want to shoot your own videos? www.SmartPhoneVideoToolkit.com

10

4. Testimonial Video

This category is pretty self-explanatory: It's your happy customers talking about their experience with your firm. These are also very easy to shoot and can be done with a couple of inexpensive lights and a smart phone. The challenge for most companies is just deciding to do it and following through. Imagine you are looking for a new dentist. You are looking at a website and you can't really differentiate one dentist from another. The dentist who has 3-10 testimonial videos on his home page, all talking about what a great experience they had in his care, will stand out from other dentists' websites without video testimonials.

Call for FREE 20 minute video consultation: 1-866-900-6969
Want to shoot your own videos? www.SmartPhoneVideoToolkit.com

11

3

BREAKING THE SEO PARADIGM
How Video Can Catapult Your Lead Generation

"The beauty of developing a video marketing plan is that you are making it easier for the viewer to be exposed to the information you are trying to communicate." – Chris Sandoval

It's common knowledge that SEO stands for search engine optimization. The problem is that for the most part SEO is dead. What I mean by that is that the days of writing content and posting it on your site, optimizing it with the right keyword phrases and the right keyword density, along with linkbacks, is pretty difficult to do. What's even less likely is to get your website to show up on Google search results, especially for competitive terms like dentist. As a result, it's much more difficult for your business to get a first page placement than it ever was before. I'm not saying it's impossible; if you're from a small town and don't have much competition, or have spent a great deal of money and effort getting your site to show up, then you might be enjoying a good placement on Google results.

Call for FREE 20 minute video consultation: 1-866-900-6969
Want to shoot your own videos? www.SmartPhoneVideoToolkit.com

12

There are only 27 positions available on the first page of the search results – meaning, if you do a search, there are only 27 actual titles, descriptions and links to websites on each page of results. Again, it's not impossible, but you also must consider the time, energy, and money it takes to get there. If you're engaging with a ranking strategy, then you know what I'm talking about.

Video is the #1 shortcut to success with lead generation
Think about a page of search results that consists of a sea of text, from top to bottom...except for one video link, conveyed by a little thumbnail picture from that video, standing out among all that text. See the image below.

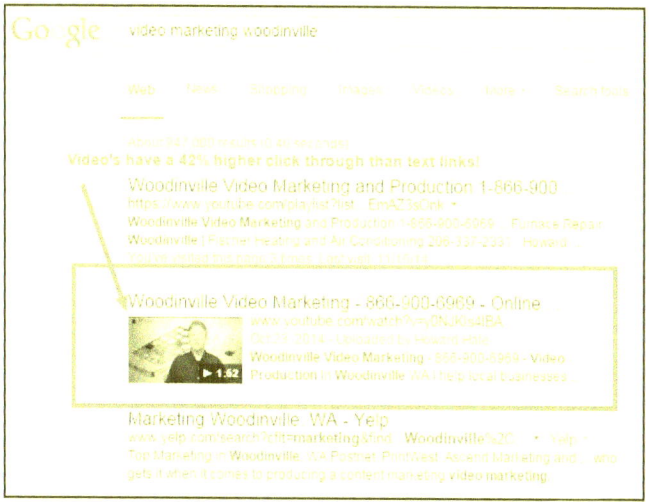

As you can see in this screen shot, taken based on the search term *"Video Marketing Woodinville"*, there's only one video showing among all that text. Which one

Call for FREE 20 minute video consultation: 1-866-900-6969
Want to shoot your own videos? www.SmartPhoneVideoToolkit.com

13

would you choose if you had a split second to make a choice? Of course it's the video, because it's visual, it's compelling and consumers are accustomed to looking at videos every day!

Video has a 42% higher click through rate than regular text links!
So let's think about this for a minute: If SEO is dead (or extremely difficult and expensive), then how should you market your business? By the way, I'm not saying don't do SEO. I'm saying that if you are on a tight budget, then you might want to consider an alternative that will give you a faster ROI than just doing SEO. If you are already engaged in SEO and it's working, then by all means keep doing it. There are no absolutes when it comes to online marketing, and as a 20 year veteran, I know that what works like the golden goose for one company may produce nothing for others.

The benefits of video have dramatically changed in recent years. It's much easier to produce quality videos, and it's much easier to get videos to rank highly in search results than ever before.
Think about what I'm saying here. You want clients to know who you are, what you do and how you do it, via the internet. The most compelling format within the internet experience is content that's delivered via video. What I'm saying that it's less expensive, easier to produce, and –get this—it can also be a standalone marketing piece that's independent of all other forms of marketing. It doesn't have to be attached to any other marketing effort in order to produce amazing results!

To summarize, you can create an effective video that will generate significant leads, you can get it to rank

Call for FREE 20 minute video consultation: 1-866-900-6969
Want to shoot your own videos? www.SmartPhoneVideoToolkit.com

14

high in the search engine results, and you can track the actual results or cost per acquisition for each and every lead. You will know exactly how your video is paying off, and your ongoing expenses are minimal when compared to all other forms of online advertising. **Now is the time to take advantage of this form of marketing before your competition does!**

Choosing the right search terms is critical
There are a variety of reasons why video can be compelling media. The approach I primarily use for lead generation is creating marketing videos based on a keyword phrase and the city location. So let's expand on the dentist example, since everyone goes to visit a dentist twice a year (I hope). If you are looking for a new dentist, then chances are you might ask a friend or family member for a referral, or you might go online and do a search for a dentist in your community. For most local businesses, the most common search phrase consists of the search term plus the city name. The other most common search phrase is the search term and/or the business name, plus the word *review*. There are a variety of terms that can be used, and some will get more traction (show up higher in Google results) than others – meaning, some terms will show up higher in Google results and not get as much traffic, while others might show up lower in Google results, but get a higher volume. Either way, it's important to have a variety of videos that focus on your top search terms plus the word *review* or the city name.

Below is an example: We'll use one of my clients – their business name is *Package It,* and are located in Seattle, Washington.

Call for FREE 20 minute video consultation: 1-866-900-6969
Want to shoot your own videos? www.SmartPhoneVideoToolkit.com

15

Here are some prime search terms for the above business:

- Packaging Supplies Woodinville
- Shipping Supplies Woodinville
- Shipping Supply Company Woodinville

If you create five videos, with keywords attached to them matching each of the five prime search phrases above, some of those videos will show up among the "sea of text" created by all the other search results. If your business shows up on the first page of Google results with a video thumbnail, it can make a huge difference in the amount of phone calls or connections you will capture from new customers.

Videos are a fraction of the cost of a Google Adwords campaign or Pay Per Click campaign.

Call for FREE 20 minute video consultation: 1-866-900-6969
Want to shoot your own videos? www.SmartPhoneVideoToolkit.com

16

4
CREATING A VIDEO STRATEGY
WHAT'S THE RIGHT STRATEGY? HOW DO YOU CREATE ONE?

"Social media sites and video go hand-in-hand, and most sites encourage video posting and sharing. The viral video opportunities are endless when you use the right strategies to create and post your videos online." – Amy Porterfield

So by now you should have a pretty good understanding of the benefits of videos, the types of keywords to use, and how videos show up in search results. We've also defined the different types of videos and their purposes. So now that you have a basic understanding (or a 50,000 foot view) of video, it's time to drill down to what type of videos you need, and why.

So, which type of video do you create? How many videos should you create? If you are a service-based business and you depend on the phone to ring, then I'd recommend the following strategy.

Hero Video - Presenting your firm's who, what, where and why
This is assuming you have a website. Creating a primary video – or what I call a hero video – is essential to converting website visitors into customers. It's your

Call for FREE 20 minute video consultation: 1-866-900-6969
Want to shoot your own videos? www.SmartPhoneVideoToolkit.com

17

"who, what, where, and why" video. This video should be between 1-3 minutes and be located near the top of your home page. The video should clearly explain your value proposition (or, the value you bring to potential customers) and contain a strong call-to-action statement. Make sure that this video prominently features your business name, your phone number, and even a special offer (if you choose to have one) on the bottom third of the screen.

Testimonial Video - Can be used for website or as marketing videos
Everyone website should have at least three testimonial videos. I'd recommend three to start with, and possibly more. Most business owners balk at this suggestion, and ignore my warnings about how important testimonials are. Think about it: what's more compelling, you (or a company representative) talking about your business, or a real satisfied customer? Then think about what's more compelling: one testimonial video or 10 testimonial videos? Anyone can get a few videos, but it's a pretty convincing message to have 10 or more videos. These

Call for FREE 20 minute video consultation: 1-866-900-6969
Want to shoot your own videos? www.SmartPhoneVideoToolkit.com

18

can be easily produced – and with some virtual support from my company, and my course *The SmartPhone Video Toolkit* – you can create videos in less than 15 minutes and upload them directly from your phone to YouTube, Facebook or even your website.

The other benefit to having this video footage is that it can and should be re-purposed in other videos. You can take one positive statement from a handful of testimonial videos and create an entirely new video. It could be part of your hero video. You'd say, "Don't believe me? Listen to what my clients have to say!" and then play the testimonial in part or in full. You can also use this footage in a marketing video: You or someone inside your firm can introduce your firm, and then you'd cut to the testimonial, playing 10 to 30 seconds of your patient saying nice things about your clinic. As you create more and more videos, they become more affordable, more visible, and will be one of your best forms of online marketing.

Compare this method with what your competitors are doing. They're posting text with the first name of their customer, and maybe an image of their customer, next to their written testimonial. That's it. It's not dynamic or interesting, and doesn't do a lot to sell their service. But you, on the other hand, have video, which becomes your magnified word-of-mouth champion, and tells your story over and over for your potential customers, clients or patients! As you can see below, video testimonials are more compelling than text.

Marketing and Sales Video
These are my favorite videos, and can be produced with a wide variety of budgets. At a minimum you want your

Call for FREE 20 minute video consultation: 1-866-900-6969
Want to shoot your own videos? www.SmartPhoneVideoToolkit.com

19

videos to have good audio and good lighting, and you

This above website shows both testimonial videos and videos from representatives within the company.

want the person on camera to tell an articulate story that the viewer can relate to. Each business owner is different, but in general, my rule of thumb is twofold.

- You should view and assess your competitor's videos, if any. You will want your videos to be noticeably better than theirs.
- If you run an auto shop, then the expectation of style is lower than if you are an attorney. What I mean by that is that no one is going to expect you to wear a suit in your auto repair shop. However, you'll want the production value to match the value that you bring to your clients and the brand that you represent. With all videos, you want to dress your best – whatever

Call for FREE 20 minute video consultation: 1-866-900-6969
Want to shoot your own videos? www.SmartPhoneVideoToolkit.com

20

counts as "best" in your industry – in neat clean clothes with tidy hair. Wearing bold colors or patterns is never a good idea unless it's part of your brand. Patterned shirts or blouses can wreak havoc with video, so always wear solid colors with no patterns.

A lead generation video can be made for a variety of styles and budgets, from completely free if produced in-house, up to possibly $1,000 to $5,000 each if outsourced. If done correctly, these videos can last for years and produce results well beyond their cost.

CAVEAT: Just because you hire an expensive videographer doesn't mean you will get the results you need or want. Hiring a professional videographer might ensure you will get a professionally produced end product, but chances are you won't get the right message with the right voice or tone of your company.

That's where a video marketing professional comes in, someone who understands your audience, your business goals and objectives, and the intention behind the creation of your video. That's very difficult for a videographer to achieve when they don't have a relationship with you or your employees, or the depth of understanding of your customers, clients or patients.

A video marketing professional will understand your needs, and find unique and cost-effective ways to accomplish the end goal.

Call for FREE 20 minute video consultation: 1-866-900-6969
Want to shoot your own videos? www.SmartPhoneVideoToolkit.com

21

5

STANDALONE OR INTEGRATION?
CREATING VIDEOS WITH (OR WITHOUT) CONSIDERING YOUR OTHER MARKETING TACTICS

"Video Marketing solidifies your online presence whilst building deep and meaningful relationships with your customers. It adds a personal touch to your brand whilst increasing your conversions!" – Lilach Bullock

There are a couple of ways to approach creating multiple videos. You can choose to integrate them into your current marketing strategy, or use them as standalone videos that generate leads for your business.

First, you have to objectively review your website to determine if you should or shouldn't integrate multiple videos into your marketing mix.

Here's my perspective. Do you need leads? Is your website improperly designed to capture leads? Or, is your site an electronic brochure that doesn't compel visitors to connect or engage with you?

Ask yourself this question: How many leads did my website generate this last month? If it's performing less

Call for FREE 20 minute video consultation: 1-866-900-6969
Want to shoot your own videos? www.SmartPhoneVideoToolkit.com

22

that you think it should, then maybe it's a deterrent. What I mean by that is that maybe your site is outdated, or it was created by a designer who doesn't have experience in marketing. Most of the sites I see today are still not doing a very good job of capturing leads. Just because you like the design of the site doesn't mean your potential customer will – and even if they do like it, does it compel them to take action and make a connection with your company?

Try not to take this personally. You may have spent a lot of your hard-earned money to develop your website. If so, and it's built with Wordpress, then chances are you can make a few changes and generate more leads or sales – even if you don't see an increase in traffic. As a conversion specialist, I help my clients with all aspects of their website and identify weaknesses. Once that's done, we can make necessary changes to get the site converting at a much higher level. Again, this skill is not common among most web designers or developers. In order to excel in this field, a marketing or conversion specialist must continue to have a relationship with the business owner, analyzing statistics and test marketing different tactics on the site.

Web designers and developers are finished helping your business once they've built the site. They don't know how successful the website becomes in achieving your goals and objectives, since they are no longer involved. They certainly don't continue to add value over time, as a marketing specialist does, as they get to know your business and how the market responds to various campaigns.

Call for FREE 20 minute video consultation: 1-866-900-6969
Want to shoot your own videos? www.SmartPhoneVideoToolkit.com

23

The following test will help you understand some of the features your website must have in order to compel visitors to connect with your business.

Please take this 2 minute quiz to determine if your site needs work!

1. Is your contact information above the fold and easily readable on the front page?
Yes _____No_____
Action Item:_____

2. Is it blatantly obvious what the purpose is of your website? (Not from your perspective, but from someone who has never seen your site.)
Write down what the purpose is

_____
Action Item:_____

3. Is there a powerful call-to-action statement that would compel visitors to connect with your business? What is the call to action?

_____
Action Item:_____

4. Is there clear and purposeful video and/or photography that your visitors can connect with, that's compelling and engages your potential customer, client or patient? Yes_____ No_____
Action Item:_____

If you answered no to some of these questions, then you might need to do some work to your website. Many businesses spend thousands of dollars each year in advertising, but their websites are not effective at

Call for FREE 20 minute video consultation: 1-866-900-6969
Want to shoot your own videos? www.SmartPhoneVideoToolkit.com

24

connecting with your potential customers. Those lost customers go searching through your competitors until they find a site that has the type of product or service they are looking for – a site that conveys trustworthiness and reliability. If your website does not convey this information instantly then it's not doing its job. Just like an employee that's not doing his or her job, you have to objectively make a decision to fix the situation or move on.

It could mean you might consider a site audit by someone unconnected to your business. Just like a financial audit, you should have someone review your site who is not a friend, family member, or your web designer to make sure it meets the needs of your customer. As the business owner, chances are you are much too close to the website to look at it objectively.

If your site is not effective at converting visitors to phone calls or connections, then no amount of traffic or advertising will fix that issue. If that's the case, then getting your site fixed should be #1 priority! You can also be working on that in parallel with the creation of videos.

If your website is not up to snuff and or you've made a conscious decision not to upgrade it for whatever reason, that's OK!

The phenomenal advantage of video is that it can be used as a standalone marketing tool. Just create your 1-3 minute video, upload it to YouTube, and add the appropriate title, description and tags for the specific keyword phrases you are targeting. And *voilà*, you have a marketing tool that tells your story better than a ton of

Call for FREE 20 minute video consultation: 1-866-900-6969
Want to shoot your own videos? www.SmartPhoneVideoToolkit.com

25

text on your website. Remember the last time you read a website all the way through? How about just the front page? I didn't think so. That's because we all scan websites for the content we're looking for. If there's a video, then we will watch that, and in 1-3 minutes we have a pretty good sense of who this company is and whether we want to do business with them. In order for your standalone videos to be effective, you need a couple of key elements to make them successful.

- A strong introduction stating what the video is about and the relationship the speaker has with the firm he or she is talking about
- Bottom (or lower) thirds. This is a banner across the bottom of the video with the company logo, phone number and other contact info. Include the website address if you're confident that the website will help with generating leads.
- The middle of the video should focus on solving one problem and convey that your firm can solve that one problem better than anyone else. Not sure what that is? Then do an informal survey of your current clients and identify what your USP (Unique Selling Proposition) is.
- The video should wrap up by stating the benefits of using your firm, how they can contact your firm, and most importantly, a strong call to action statement so there is no confusion that you would like to meet them and have them use your business.
- I strongly recommend some compelling offer that's unique, so you can track the success of your video campaigns.

Don't forget to add an ending title showing all your

Call for FREE 20 minute video consultation: 1-866-900-6969
Want to shoot your own videos? www.SmartPhoneVideoToolkit.com

26

contact information. A music track playing in the background is also a nice touch and adds a more professional and engaging quality to your video.

Call for FREE 20 minute video consultation: 1-866-900-6969
Want to shoot your own videos? www.SmartPhoneVideoToolkit.com

27

6
GETTING IT DONE
CREATING VIDEO IN-HOUSE VS. HIRING A VIDEOGRAPHER

"The sheer cost of video production has come down to a point where there are no barriers to entry. Buyers have devices that can play videos with them at all times… [and] are engaging in 100% more information year-over-year before they make a buying decision." – Joe Pulizzi

Creating a script or outline
You can use a script or an outline; choose what feels right to you. I recommend creating a script and practicing with it, but then not using it when you start filming (see below). Writing the script out and doing a table read will help you to get some sentences and word choices rolling around. Reading a script word-for-word on camera sounds really bad, and unless you are a professional, the viewer can totally tell that you are reading. If you do go this route, then a teleprompter is in order. If you don't use one, you will look shifty-eyed to the viewer as you look slightly off-camera to read the script.

The other option is to prepare some questions for someone to ask you. Just answer the questions while looking into the camera. This works very well, and you

Call for FREE 20 minute video consultation: 1-866-900-6969
Want to shoot your own videos? www.SmartPhoneVideoToolkit.com

28

can do jump cuts to remove the interviewer's voice in post-production.

If you plan on doing a video with a voiceover, then you really have it made. It's super easy to read your script and cut out unwanted sections as needed in post-production.

While these videos can rank high in the search engine results, they are not quite as compelling. When doing testimonial videos of customers I'd recommend having a list of questions to ask so that your happy customer isn't stressed about having to make something up. These can be shot slightly off camera and don't need to be perfect. What you are looking for with this and all videos is for them to be authentic!

Practice being on camera
There are several options when it comes to getting your video created. Either way, you need to practice! First off, I'd suggest practicing with your smart phone. I've videoed hundreds of people on camera, and I can tell who has and who hasn't practiced in front of a camera or smart phone. If you are hiring a professional video crew and you aren't prepped and ready to go, then you might have to pay for a reshoot and that can be costly, take longer, and be frustrating to the crew you hire. A great guide to creating videos, writing scripts and shooting videos is my book **The SmartPhone Video Toolkit**. See the resource guide at the end of this book for more information.

Shooting footage on your own
If you are comfortable shooting video, then by all means do it. Once you have some footage that you think is

Call for FREE 20 minute video consultation: 1-866-900-6969
Want to shoot your own videos? www.SmartPhoneVideoToolkit.com

29

usable, you can have someone edit the footage, put in titles, and add some music. I highly recommend that my clients stay involved in this process, especially for testimonial videos. It's the only true way you will get both the quality and quantity of videos you need to dominate your competition.

Creating video in-house vs. hiring a videographer

There's nothing wrong with creating your own videos in house, provided you can create the quality that your customers expect. If you need support getting your skills up to speed, then by all means you can hire a videographer to help shoot the videos and an editor to edit them. Sometimes you can have one person do both of these services, along with uploading them to YouTube or posting them on your website.

As a full service firm, I like it when a client wants to get involved – either to offload some of the effort that goes into the creation of the video, or to add some creativity. At the end of the day, you want your videos to be an extension of the voice of your business. It should attract your perfect target audience and compel them to do business with you. The inverse is also true: you want to repel clients that are not your ideal target audience and that you don't want to work with. I have a variety of techniques that I have successfully used to deter problem customers.

The hybrid approach

You can also hire a professional to film you for the introduction and conclusion of the video. You then provide the client testimonials for the middle, and the end product is a great way to create a professional video and tell a compelling story that's authentic.

Call for FREE 20 minute video consultation: 1-866-900-6969
Want to shoot your own videos? www.SmartPhoneVideoToolkit.com

30

If you decide to hire a firm to create your videos, then consider a few things prior to making your decision:

- If you get three bids, you will get three prices.
- Experience in creating videos does not equate to videos that will rank high, appeal to your target audience or generate real leads.
- Video production or creation and video marketing are two separate skill sets.
- Make sure whoever you hire has a policy that doesn't charge you marketing fees for a given month if you don't show up on the front page of search results.
- I highly recommend using a call tracking number so that you know for a fact your videos are generating leads and revenue. This is a practice I use for all marketing campaigns to determine what works and what doesn't, so I can reallocate financial resources to what does work. Using a unique telephone number and receiving a weekly report telling you which video is working is the only viable way to track results.
- While creating a highly polished video for your website could be a great move, make sure you understand your audience and that they will appreciate a high production value video. Some customers could be put off if it's too perfect.

The benefits of having video as a marketing tactic
Hopefully you have discovered by now that video is a great tactic for lead generation, and you're currently considering taking advantage of the low hanging fruit of online marketing and customer acquisition.

Call for FREE 20 minute video consultation: 1-866-900-6969
Want to shoot your own videos? www.SmartPhoneVideoToolkit.com

There are other benefits to having video:
- It separates you from the competition and differentiates you from them.
- It can extend your brand and strengthen it at the same time.
- It can explain who you are, what you do and how you do it more easily than any other form of marketing.

Creating your own video with your smart phone
Video can be the most compelling feature on your website. In seconds, a visitor can make the decision to use or not to use your service or buy your product. An engaging video can make all the difference in that decision – and the same can be said for the rest of your site. Creating and uploading videos is easier than ever before, and videos are becoming an integral part of all business website marketing. Businesses that embrace video going forward and leverage it will win a greater share of customers, clients or patients.

The challenge for most small businesses is finding the right resources to tell your story while maintaining your brand – and without breaking your budget. You need a persuasive video that will cause the viewer to take action. The approach to video creation that I outline in this book is an iterative process. Start creating videos sooner, rather than later, and focus your energy on quantity vs. quality to start. I'm not saying you should give up on high-quality videos. I'm saying you can begin using the iterative process I will outline in this book and, as your skills develop, the quality of your videos will naturally improve. You will discover resources inside and outside your company, and you will hone your company's message as you go, all of

Call for FREE 20 minute video consultation: 1-866-900-6969
Want to shoot your own videos? www.SmartPhoneVideoToolkit.com

32

which will improve your video content over time. Of course, you can use your budget to hire an expensive production company to make a slick video, but that still won't ensure that the video will turn out to your satisfaction, or that the video will connect with your target audience. Nor will it guarantee the "shelf-life" of your expensive video. The goal of my book, the **SmartPhone Video Toolkit** is to help you generate effective video content quickly, and to engage in an ongoing process that will create videos that will engage your audience.

An amazing percentage of adults in the United States watch videos. If your website doesn't have a video, your business could be left behind. I'm not saying that people won't choose your service because you don't have a video, but they may be more inclined to choose what you have to offer if you have a video that effectively describes your product or service.

You may be thinking to yourself, "I don't want to be seen on video," or "I'm totally uncomfortable with it." If so, the video doesn't have to be about you. Whether you're a solopreneur or a large business, the goal is to reach your customers, not to make yourself into a celebrity spokesperson. You can generate great video content by focusing on your team, your product, or your customers' experience.

For some businesses, a personal touch and attracting visitors to your website to get to know and trust you is the most powerful calling card you can employ. You may bring in many kinds of people to support your effort to create video content, and you don't have to spend a lot of money to do so. In fact, low-cost videos

Call for FREE 20 minute video consultation: 1-866-900-6969
Want to shoot your own videos? www.SmartPhoneVideoToolkit.com

33

can be more believable to your audience and can create a deeper, more personal connection with them. I created the **SmartPhone Video Toolkit** to help business owners and nonprofits produce higher-quality videos with genuinely compelling messages that can connect customers with products and services.

No matter how great or small your marketing budget might be, I highly recommend that everyone interested in creating videos start by using a smart phone.

An iPhone, Android, or any other kind of smart phone is perfectly adequate for the task at hand. All are easy to use and widely available. Many people are surprised to discover that they already have such a versatile and effective means of video production in their pocket. Many of the memorable videos you've watched on the web, whether it was an adorable pet video or a criminal caught in the act, were shot with equipment on par with, or below, the quality you can expect to get from your smart phone. Today's smart phone camera technology is perfect for creating inexpensive, effective videos, especially if you take the time to follow the steps I'm going to give you. Working with an easy-to-use camera allows you to focus on the elements of production that will quickly improve the quality of your videos as you become more and more adept. A solid script, good audio, good lighting, and a succinct message that binds the video together are all facets that we will discuss here, in addition to getting the most out of a camera that slips into your pocket.

Call for FREE 20 minute video consultation: 1-866-900-6969
Want to shoot your own videos? www.SmartPhoneVideoToolkit.com

34

7
GEAR GUIDE
TO CREATE YOUR OWN VIDEOS

"Stop thinking of 'video marketing' as this separate entity that is optional for your business. Video is an effective form of communication that needs to be integrated into each and every aspect of your existing marketing efforts." – James Wedmore

Getting specialized gear for your smart phone is fairly easy if you buy it on Amazon. For the most part, you can't just go down to your local electronics or camera store and pick it up. The same goes for other video equipment. While you can buy a digital single-lens reflex (DSLR) camera at your local big-box store, the other accessories – such as lighting, tripods, and the like – may not be available in your local area. I live in Seattle and most of what I need for shooting videos with my DSLR or my iPhone is not available in local stores.

I have some cool tools for you! I must confess, one of my favorite things to do is to buy new toys—I mean, *gear*—to test out and see if it makes a difference in the quality of my work, and to see which tools have value for my clients and readers.

Call for FREE 20 minute video consultation: 1-866-900-6969
Want to shoot your own videos? www.SmartPhoneVideoToolkit.com

35

All the gear you need to create professional videos are on my website (above) in my Amazon Store. www.HaleSyndicate.com

When it comes to shooting video, where else can you get a video camera for a few hundred dollars that shoots, edits, and uploads directly to YouTube? I always start by searching on Amazon when I want to invest in a new piece of equipment, even if I don't necessarily plan to buy online, because it's very helpful to see how people rate a particular product. A lot of times, it's hard to tell the quality of something unless

Call for FREE 20 minute video consultation: 1-866-900-6969
Want to shoot your own videos? www.SmartPhoneVideoToolkit.com

36

you read about the experiences of other consumers.

Most of the products I mention are listed on my website at www.HaleSyndicate.com/gear. And in the interest of full disclosure, I do make a small percentage from my affiliate program with Amazon. But, trust me, I don't get rich from this. It's designed to help you find all the gear you need in one spot. What I do make goes back into the creation of my semi-annual gear guide to show you what the latest tools are, to make your project easier and improve quality.

The Gear Guide is FREE with the purchase of my book, The SmartPhone Video Toolkit.

Call for FREE 20 minute video consultation: 1-866-900-6969
Want to shoot your own videos? www.SmartPhoneVideoToolkit.com

37

8
CONCLUSION

"Video marketing is, without a doubt, one of the biggest reasons I've been able to create a multiple six-figure business online." – Katie Freiling

For obvious reasons, I'm a pretty big proponent of video. I've seen it transform businesses and make a connection with an audience second only to a live interaction with a real human being. Video truly is the one thing that connects customers, clients and patients with your business. It's doesn't matter if you are a physician, attorney, real estate agent, consultant or any other type of business. A well thought out and executed video can make a huge impact on your bottom line and how the general public sees you. Commit to making a video for your business and I'm confident that you will not only see results from the video, but you will be proud to post it on your website and all your social sites, and send out the link via email to current clients and potential clients!

As I like to say, **Life is Short, Hit Record!**

-Howard Hale

Call for FREE 20 minute video consultation: 1-866-900-6969
Want to shoot your own videos? www.SmartPhoneVideoToolkit.com

RESOURCES

Contact Info for Howard Hale
Call my toll free number at 1-866-900-6969

Email Howard at:
book@halesyndicate.com

**To learn more about my book, please go to
www.SmartPhoneVideoToolkit.com or do a search on
Amazon for "Howard Hale" to see the books I've
published.**

My YouTube channel
https://www.youtube.com/user/hhaleh

My Facebook page
https://www.facebook.com/pages/Hale-Syndicate

My websites:
http://SmartPhoneVideoToolkit.com
http://HaleSyndicate.com

Call for FREE 20 minute video consultation: 1-866-900-6969
Want to shoot your own videos? www.SmartPhoneVideoToolkit.com

39

BOOKING HOWARD FOR YOUR EVENTS

If you're looking to train some of your employees or students to be videographers, I can help. I have a wide variety of curricula that cover all aspects of creating video using mobile devices, and I can also advise on what gear to purchase based on the needs of your organization.

If you need someone to speak at your event or to your organization about creating video, I provide this service. I can speak on a variety of topics – from the personal aspect of connecting using video, to the technical aspects of how to create compelling video.

Shooting video the first time can be the biggest challenge. Once you overcome some of the initial concerns or fears you have about it, it becomes second nature, and your ease with the process will grow. Whatever your purpose is, I can help your organization through those initial hurdles and get your workflow running smoothly so that you can increase the quality and quantity of videos.

I can also help facilitate using video at events and doing multicamera shoots with live streaming, for example, as a method to report on trade shows or action happening live in the field. This work can be done by using combinations of smart phones, tablets or other mobile devices. Whatever your needs are, I can help support them personally or refer you to a specialist so that you get the right expert advice that fits your goals and objectives.

LIVE CLASSES I TEACH

Most of my classes are based on my book and the videos I create. I'm always looking for the shortest path to creating videos that reach out to the viewer and create connection. Taking a hands-on class and learning live is the most effective, kinetic way to get experience in creating great looking videos. It also helps to have your gear right here so you can find out any issues you might have in your workflow. Not everything runs perfectly the first time. It's those moments that you struggle with where the best learning often occurs. Having a guide who helps you through the process and leads you into and out of the areas that you are challenged with can be a valuable, enriching experience and save you a lot of time.

Here are just a few of the classes/workshops I teach. If you don't see what you need, please contact me.

- **Cool Videos That Create Hot Sales** – A 1-day event on creating sales videos for your business or organization with the goal to simply convert more viewers to sales.
- **The SmartPhone Video Toolkit Intensive** – A 3-day event on all aspects of creating quality video with your mobile device. You will go

Call for FREE 20 minute video consultation: 1-866-900-6969
Want to shoot your own videos? www.SmartPhoneVideoToolkit.com

41

home with the knowledge and skills to create, edit, and upload quality videos.

* **Video Partner Program: The Video Makers Symposium and Mastermind** – A 2-3 day event, this program is designed for authors and speakers who would like to integrate their wisdom and brilliance with the video creation process. We work as a team and create a compelling program that engages students on a whole new level.

Call for FREE 20 minute video consultation: 1-866-900-6969
Want to shoot your own videos? www.SmartPhoneVideoToolkit.com

42

SPECIAL OFFER!
PURCHASE MY BOOK AND GET THE
FOLLOWING FOR FREE!

If you want to create your own videos, get my book for less than the price of a latte – plus everything you see below for FREE!
Go to Amazon and type in Howard Hale or
Type this in your web browsers address bar->
http://amzn.to/1pDnip9

Call for FREE 20 minute video consultation: 1-866-900-6969
Want to shoot your own videos? www.SmartPhoneVideoToolkit.com

43